Village Mechanics

Abigail Carl-Klassen

FLOWERSONG
PRESS

About the Bougainvillea Poetry Prize

The Bougainvillea Poetry Prize is awarded to a poetry collection that addresses issues concerning the poor, workers, the underclass, financial insecurity, working conditions, inequity, and precarity. It promotes work that illuminates, narrates, or champions the lives of working-class people as they navigate the world.

The prize honors the memory of Irma (1939-2010) and Alfonso (1938-2021) Gomez of Brownsville, Texas—Mexican-Americans who raised seven children while working in various jobs such as cashier, ice worker, homemaker, truck driver, migrant farmworker, painter, and custodian, among many others.

The prize's name is a direct reference to the bougainvillea, an ornamental plant with protective adaptations such as thorns and skin-irritating sap, frequently found in the lower Rio Grande Valley of Texas. The name also references the Bougainvillea Housing Development—a 50-unit project in downtown Brownsville, with an average living area of 700 square feet per unit—where the Gomez children were raised.

Winners of the Bougainvillea Poetry Prize

2025: Abigail Karl-Klassen, *Village Mechanics*

Contents

This flood of convergences…in the guise of the commonplace
Édouard Glissant

I. Village Mechanics

Village Mechanics: Return

In 1922 5,000 Low-German speaking Old Colony Menno-
nites immigrated to Mexico from Canada at the invitation
of President Álvaro Obregón in the wake of the Mexican
Revolution. They settled in the northern state of Chihuahua
and built separatist communities known as Darpe (villages)
far removed from the rest of Mexican society, both in distance
and culture. Today there are more than 50,000 Low-German
speaking Mennonites living in Chihuahua, some of whom
continue to live in near isolation, while others have integrat-
ed, at various levels, into Mexican society. Over the years,
many Mennonites born in Mexico later immigrated to Texas,
Kansas, Belize, Paraguay and Bolivia, while others returned to
Canada.

Mumkje Froese's English Lesson

I don't

have an accent. Your ears

       have an
       accent.

The Mennonite Game

What do you call a bad Mennonite
poet? Corny Reimer. Why don't Mennonites

have sex standing up? It might lead
to dancing. A Mexican and a Mennonite

are in a car together. Who is
driving? Border Patrol. What happens

when you take one Mennonite
fishing? He drinks all your beer. Do you

know how copper wire was invented? A Mennonite mom
gave her kids a penny and told

them to share. What is a Mennonite ethical
dilemma? Free condoms and beer. What happens

when you take two Mennonites fishing? They don't drink
any of your beer. Why don't Mennonite women

wear sleeveless dresses? They can't
bear arms. What is an Amish woman's secret

fantasy? Two Mennonite. How many Mennonites does it
take to change a light bulb?

Change? How do you break
Mennonites' necks? Walk around their trucks.

Thoughts Driving West Out of Seminole, Texas

> *Behold how good and how pleasant it is for brethren to*
> *dwell together in unity*
> **Psalm 133:1**

God made West Texas flat so people can see the back
    of their own heads. And the way the horizon cuts

behind rows of houses with metal roofs and green
    doors and fields that look the same as everyone

else's. Except. A little straighter. Maybe. Trees
    dirt drives. Saplings pulled straight by ropes

staked on both sides. Striped shirts and solid
    dresses of all sizes flap during the day. The lines

empty at night. The Village exists because it is
invisible and wayward English can't tell

the difference between in and out of the country
roads that connect the Village. They never see

what is. In plain view. The Village did not always exist
but began when the first person was born again

again. Suspended between future and past
at the same time. And never. A cross

between here and there. Village and World. One real,
one a mirage, both in the desert, determined

by a choice. Mennonites are not born
they are recreated and each one must

decide: the old ways or the world
that doesn't understand the choosing.

Walking in Colonia Rubio: Old Colony Mennonite Settlements, Chihuahua, Mexico

Laundry day. Monday and Friday. By hand. I smell the Sun
soap powder as I crunch the path, dusted and packed flat
by steel wheels of un-painted trailers and propelled

by bare-backed mares, in my black strapped huaraches
Grösspapa bought in Casas Grandes. Threads gape
from my stockings, hen-pecked while the rooster chuckles

and I kick him away from the hem of my dress, jagged,
since I stitched it myself for the first time. Flowers cut
from the same fabric my mother and sisters bought, fifteen

yards at the dietsche Wal-mart, to match our new straw
hats. Wide ribbons around the brims so we could tell them
apart from the ones our brothers wore with their striped

kjnpse Hamd and coveralls. Before my brother nailed
his outhouse closed after our father said he was going to
hell, because my nephews pissed inside, buckets, heavy, well

water on green tile. Before we snuck out, under the summer
moon to play volleyball outside the neighbor's barn, until
preachers, in black coats and Bekjse, split and gutted our ball

with a crowbar and stomped the Devil (a portable radio
that only played corridos from Cuauhtémoc and weather
from El Valle) with their boots and Die Biebel. We could

not decipher their shapes, but we knew they demanded
silence. Its corpse sagged on the clothes line and I walk
that line to recover stains cranked from the rusted handle,

where I crouched over a trough of Wranglers (bought once
a year, cheap in El Paso) and polyester aprons we ironed
Tuesdays before tractors had rubber tires. And before I smoked

cheap cigarettes with wild Mennonite boys who drove flat-bed
pick- ups. And drank warm Tecates, while they turned their
eyes from our waist high panties, strung like flags of surrender.

Chupacabra Summer: Seminole, Texas, 1998

Leah's neighbors tied a goat to the clothesline behind their house. The rope stretched so far; he could stick his nose into the dirt piled high on top of an underground cellar that hadn't been opened since before the Mennonites came to Seminole. When we were thirteen, we dug with our hands for an afternoon and uncovered the door, a thin sheet of tarnished metal, edges jagged and bowed in the middle. We pried the latch open with a broken PVC pipe and there was nothing inside except for spiders. Hundreds. Daddy long legs mostly harmless. Leah's Aunt Tina who lived in the Village outside town kept goats in a pen and said they were so dumb they would slice up their insides eating cans. Only the neighbor goat survived because he couldn't reach the rust on the side of the dumpster. That summer we sat on the back steps and snapped pictures in the dark, peace signs and bunny ears first. Bubble gum bursts on the tips of our noses. Lips smacked and glossed clear. Tongues thrust out at Leah's brother Daniel and his Engalander girlfriend, red lipstick and feathered bangs. Her hand in the back pocket of his Wranglers as they pressed against his pickup truck. Mom's coming, we would yell, just to watch them jump, but they still let us come to Sonic with them sometimes, ice creams to keep us quiet. While we watched Southern Baptist and Mennonite teens in tank tops and tight pants lean out windows of moving cars to see if they could cruise the drag in a silver power stroke diesel. Daniel's girlfriend tried to teach us how tie knots in cherry stems with our teeth, but we never could. Most nights we stayed behind, Tweety Bird pajama shirts stretched over our knees, waist-length hair soaking our backs as we sat on the floor and thumbed glossy 10mm prints. Hands over our mouths, faces in pillows to smother fits of giggles. Darkness behind us, the goat ready to charge. Eyes fluorescent.

Watching Las Reinas: Rubio, Chihuahua, 1990s

I never got to be in the certamen
for the beauty queens even though I
was nominated every year since I
started school with the Mexicans. I bet

I would have won too—everyone here
is in love with rubias. I just got to
bake cupcakes for the fundraiser. I
didn't march for Independence Day

or dance folklórico either. My parents
wrote letters saying it was against
our religion, but I still had to help
decorate during art class. I loved

cutting out hearts and flowers for
the floats and getting to use spray
glitter. No matter how hard I tried
I always ended up covered in sparkles.

Yoder Family Singers World Tour 2002: Seminole, Texas

Only a man who used to be Amish would wear a carnival
meets Elton John shirt that shimmers while he picks

the twelve string that he hid inside his parents' barn before
he left Garnett, Kansas. And moved to Paris,

Texas, with thirty-two dollars in his pocket, a day labor
mechanic before he was called a good news prophet. Singing

southern gospel songs to Mennonites who have a weakness
for old-time bluegrass music. That is new

to them because it used to be forbidden. Snaps
strain to shut over his chest hair, saluting

the women's side of the church. Good girls cast
their eyes down because their fathers and brothers

always button above the collar. Unless they are
working in the fields alone where they know women

can't see them. But the worldly Mejjalles, who hide
underwire and pink plastic razors in their drawers

stifle silent laughs into hands clasped over their exposed
tongues. Raising unplucked eyebrows at the Junges

slouching in the men's benches. Thinking of the last
time they saw shirtless young men, lying in the bed

of a diesel stroke pickup truck Saturday night,
but now, bewildered by flesh exposed at the front

of the church. Yoder's wife testifies, Tammy Faye lashes
blurred by the Holy Spirit. Bedazzled

jean jacket pulled tight across her scooped
t-shirt. Silver hoops and aquamarine crosses

smack against her neck, catching her bleach
blonde perm, roots uncovered. Hips

clang against her bangles while she stamps black
pumps. Square-tipped acrylic pointing up.

A Warning to Every Mennonite Waitress in Mexico

She's a menonita que no puede
bailar. Not one foot in front
of the other, paso a paso, no

corridos, cumbias, salsas or what
evers. Her hips, stiff and untouched
angles jabbing through her polyester

dress, pulled up so she could show
off her lower calves, or at least
that's her excuse when she stumbles.

Slow seductress, but still, she tries to
flirt behind a batch of bread and dreams
of boys in cowboy boots and Skoal

tin imprints rising the seams of their
Wrangler jeans. Sliding across hard
wood floors, she remembers the Devil

music she heard in Cuauhtémoc, looks
behind her to make sure no one will
see when she steps into the fire.

Rapture

You spent more time in front of the mirror than with the Lord this morning. You want to be there when Jesus comes back, your shirt, short, tramp stamp flash of flesh when you raise your hands to praise him? Jesus is watching you. Hands out of your pants. You won't think it's funny—all alone when he gets back. Jesus is coming. Look busy. Remember. You want to be on bottom when Jesus gets back. And Jesus is listening in the shower. He's going to enter the atmosphere and break

in, to expose your nakedness to everybody in glory. He's gonna snatch you by your severed umbilical cord into that last chance escape hatch of the universe. The cracked insides of the million millennia of supernova blasts, that whirling dervish kaleidoscope of Technicolor convergence. Dark matter dripping off your back into evaporation, and your glistening body always reaching up—

Temporary People

For Judy—whose parents followed the harvest

Gin means that you start down south and diesel
dye your stripper, that International Harvester,
through barbed wire, the only thing between

Amarillo and the Northern Lights (besides all
those cans of Keystone Light stacked up into
a piss beer altar at the Black Diamond. Where

roughnecks are discounted and truckers are
welcome to squeeze as many men into a
sleeper as there are naked ladies on mud

flaps). Gin means that every new atmosphere tastes
like the last turn in the white horizon that was
yellow in April and May. But under the winter

moon she'll be naked. That is, if the combines
don't heat up too much. Sometimes metal sparks
diesel and diesel sparks cotton and you

heard that in the Bible Armageddon is a field on
 fire. Melting holes in your only pair of steel toed
boots, but is just a lit matchstick for a second

when seen from the interstate. The same as agent
orange. Breath dusted through a blanket not made
in America, where temporary people work

twelve on and sleep twelve off, on the back
room floor. Fingers taped. Blisters, bones
exposed so you can drive again tomorrow.

The Schekbenjel Goes for a Ride: Mennonite Settlements, Chihuahua, Late 1980s

I had me two girlfriends once. In different Darps but still close enough to walk. I'd visit one Sunday after church, then I'd visit the other one Sunday after supper. After I started working, just a Schekbenjel, but still making some dough, I saved up. Bought me a motorbike. Thought I was hot stuff cruisin' in and out of the Villages. I could go to a bunch of them now since I wasn't just walkin'. The bike was small but I was real fast. Kicking up dust like nobody's business. One Sunday, I'd blown off both of my girlfriends because I wanted to ride around. Feel some real power. So, I drove way out to this Darp I'd never been to before. Out in the middle of nowhere, but I could already tell they liked to party. Pick–up trucks parked all over the yard. And the music was pumpin' real loud. A bunch of boys and girls runnin' around. All these smokje Me'jalles. I mean real nice lookin'. So, I slowed down to take it all in. These tough lookin' bros were hollerin' and wavin' their beer cans around. Yellin' for me to gun it. So, I did. Tore it up to the end of the road and whipped back into their driveway. Doin' ninety easy. Then ripped some donuts into the gravel. All the girls were screamin' and laughin'. So, I burnt some more rubber. Laid it out real thick 'til some dudes jumped out of a truck cab and started slappin' me on the back sayin' bro, that's rad come drink with us. I was about to take my helmet off and grab a cold one, but then I saw both my girlfriends sittin' on a picnic table. Carryin' on like they was best friends. Painted and pressed up against some ugly ass cowboys.

Thriftway Run

Last Sunday after church Lena Froese stuffed her cart with heavy cream, potatoes, and chicken stock to make Sommabarsch with her daughters for the family gathering at her sister's place. Sixty or so if everyone showed. Rows of wheat rolls cooling on racks. Two five-gallon buckets of ice cream in the garage freezer. Liters of Fanta and Dr. Pepper on the counter. Ham bone from last week's butchering already simmering. Spice ball sputtering. Crushed. Bay leaves, star anise, beet greens, dill and sorrel. Any herb growing above ground before winter. That could be thrown into a Gröpe. In the old country. The first Old Colony. Flat like Seminole. Green like Steinbach. Winds, fierce, like Cuauhtémoc. When she bent down in the parking lot to unload the plastic bags, the trunk of her Suburban sprang open and smashed her glasses against her eyelids, jolting bones in the bridge of her nose into a trickle of salt water blood that stung the cracks in her lips. But before Anna, her oldest and already married, could reach into her purse to call the doctor, silent and jaw unhinged, Lena plunged her thumb and forefinger upward and straightened it back with one single crack.

Self-Portraits with the Flower Women (Las Mujeres Flores1, Yo, and Eunice Adorno)

1.

One time I watched Willy Zacharias' mom lift a refrigerator above her shoulders and into the bed of an F150. Engalander teenage boys, friends of her son, stood stupid, slack jawed with a dolly and bungee cords in their fists, as she swatted them back with her neck. Wiping her hands in the pleats of her dress, she tipped her head back, pursed her lips and said, well, guess I'll get supper started.

2.

After supper, the men talked in the living room while Leah and I scraped the last bits of baked potato into the trash. Stacked towers of flowered plates on the counter. Filled the sinks and turned on the coffee maker. Three scoops of Shure-fine regular, not decaf. My turn to wash. Her turn to rinse and dry. Flicking soap bubbles in her ear, I ducked as she splashed back. Leah's mom, Mumkje Dyck, looked up from her dust pan. Careful girls, if your stomach gets wet when you wash dishes your husband is going to be lazy. When Mumkje looked back down, Leah stuck out her tongue.

3.

Steel pop as we soaked sausage casings. And spread them to
dry. The coffee pot sputtered. Josiah must have killed the pig
dead with just one shot. Mumkje Froese nodded, sharpening
her knives as her sons hung the hairless mass up by the hooves
and split the ribs with an electric saw. Hog, headless, hooked
and swinging from the shop ceiling. I knocked on the propane
tank under the Gröpe where we would boil the fat, kidneys
and heart. And any other scrap meat. Sounds like it's full.
Should be able to run it most of the day. Mumkje handed me
a wooden post. You can stir it first. I'll need to watch it once
it gets thicker. Grüewen, pig crystals. Spread on top of hot
rolls the morning after the slaughter, while hams packed with
salt hang inside the barn. She sipped her coffee and smiled.
Neita, she called to the woman testing the vacuum sealer. Tell
the rest of the ladies they can come over now and bring their
husbands too. It's processing time.

4.

The Trajchmoaka's trailer had a red 5 spray-painted on the side. Two boys with trucker caps and pants tucked into their boots chased each other around number 7. Boards nailed over window holes of number 11. We didn't have to knock. We watched her watching us from the kitchen window. She ground down her cigarette, shifted her Duäk, and reached into her black slacks for another bobby pin. While she pressed Leah's vertebrae with open palms, I sat in the corner watching a telenovela flicker on a black and white TV with the sound turned off. Photographs of her dead husband between the rabbit ears. Do you want her to massage your back? She says it's only five dollars.

5.

Mennoniten in Mexiko 1922-1962. Leah's grandma is in that book. Smiling next to a washing machine in her parent's front yard. Barefoot. Hand on the crank. The same age as us. The first time we looked. A sleepwalker for life. Every night for two years before she got married, she woke up standing under the moon. A full bucket sloshing, on her nightdress, drops of milk.

6.

When Zeusa brought The Mennonites2to Taunte Neita, they sat at the kitchen table sipping Tim Hortons and munching on Faspa. She waited for Neita to smile when she recognized the Village where she grew up. But instead, she threw the book on the floor. Look at us! He should be ashamed at the way that he shows our people! He must have found every poor, desperate Mennonite in Mexico and taken pictures!

7.

Neita told a story once. About when she was newly married. She, her sister, brother-in-law and husband all stuffed into a single cab truck. For their yearly trip to El Paso. Shifter stuck between her knees as her husband wound around the mountains. Halfway between Cuauhtémoc and Juárez. At a bodega. Middle of Nowhere. The men stopped to stretch. And pay for the outhouse. The women stayed inside the truck cracking windows. Wiping sweat from their temples. The men came back. Frosted. Glass bottles pressed to their lips. Neither of them said a word. Jamming the keys in the ignition her husband reached between her legs. To shift into first. She watched the last of the brown liquid slide down his throat.

8.

A strip of dough hung past my elbow and swung before I pinched it in half between my thumb and forefinger. And twirled the two ends together with my other hand. Slow, but with the patience of a sixteen-year-old. Mumkje Froese looked up from her rows of baking sheets and laughed, if you want to get married soon you have to make Kringel like this. Two flips of the wrist. Each notch in the braid exactly the same. No thumbprints.

9.

In Redekop's Old Colony Mennonites3 Appendix I read a footnote about two Mennonite women who became prostitutes among Mexicans. An apparently mentally marginal woman and another who was considered brilliant.

10.

Long hair is a woman's glory. Zeusa's shorn close to the scalp. Star tattoo poking her ear lobe. At work her empty gauges slack. Facing bills behind the teller desk. Jappa turned seventeen this week but she didn't see it. Until he snuck away from the high school at lunch and parked his truck in the drive-thru. She squinted through the tinted glass as he scrawled on a deposit slip. Pressed send and rocketed the tube toward her. I miss you Zeusa. Mom is wrong but maybe someday she'll get over it and let you come back. She doesn't say much but I know she feels bad. Slipping the note back with a click, she bit her lip knowing that she wouldn't hear him laugh when he popped the top. A lollipop rainbow bursting from the tube.

1. *Las Mujeres Flores*, published in 2010, is a collection of photographs taken by Eunice Adorno in Old Colony settlements in Mexico.

2. Larry Towell's collection of photographs of Mennonite migrant workers in Mexico and Canada published in 2000.

3. Redekop's *Old Colony Mennonites*, published in 1969, is one of the definitive ethnographictexts about the Old Colony communities in Mexico.

Sonnet for Tobacco Pickers

Everyone knows who picks tobacco. Hands
stained and cracked for the season. Saturday
nights my oldest brother and I soak our hands in
bowls of bleach water. It burns and still doesn't
match the rest of our skin, but it's close enough.
We can't do it every day because there'd be too
much blood, but for Sundays it's worth it so the
girls at church won't notice as much. That's what
we tell ourselves as we pour pink water down the
sink. Fingers still sting the next morning as we
whip metal cans from our Wrangler seat pockets
and dip wet combs into chunks of hair wax. We
lean back, thumbs locked in belt loops.
Reflections smiling.

Lilies of the Field

Mumkje Neufeld flipped her clip-on shades as late
afternoon rainbows refracted off her glasses on to her dress,

lemon, like cotton blossoms. The last Devil's Claw of the day
drooping from her blade, she rested the hoe against her hip

and squeezed warm drops against her lips before passing the
bottle across the row to her daughters, four Mejalles pulling

at their oversized shirts and dusting their hands against the
seams of their jeans. Next year Margie would be sixteen. Old

enough to join a spraying crew. Born in Lamesa, Texas, and
legal to work in America, she would be paid by the hour and

not by the row. Sitting under the shade of a diesel engine,
she would chug away to power spray streams of RoundUp

PowerMax and Dual Magnum on to fields three towns over.
Shaking her head, Mumkje dragged her hand toward her

temple, but before she could press her straw hat back,
she thought she saw the sand shift around her ankles. Steel

raised without hesitation, she stumbled back from the staff
still shaking.Blood spattered on her cracked flats, the snake's

severed head turned upward. Jaw unhinged.
Ready to strike.

Divine Healing

Mumkje Dyck goes to Juárez every three weeks for salt
pills to thin the blood crystals under her skin, crushed
chiles to deflate her swollen heart vessels and wonder
oil for the rheumatoid arthritis beginning to curl

her fingers like Kjielkje noodles before they are pressed flat.
Mumkje is afraid
to drive in the city so she waits until Saturday
when her husband Abe, who witches for water

in the desert and drills wells for farmers, can
take her. Abe has been driving since he could reach the
tractor pedals and his Spanish is better since he used to work
as a day laborer, getting drunk in Cuauhtémoc

until he received a vision from the Lord, who spoke, over
the fire and the demons and the rock music, *Abe, you will
be dead in two days, if you don't stop drinking.* Now when he
goes back to Mexico he knocks

Zoot in an Allsup's cup and scatters the shells
at a hundred miles an hour over Guadalupe Pass, while
he and Mumkje listen to Gloria Gaither shout *Holy Ghost
Power*, foreheads alight with oil, hands lifting in prayer.

Neighbor

The screen door smacked against the frame as she let herself
in after a couple of soft knocks. And a nod of acknowledg-
ment from Leah, still a teenager then, her ponytail slapping
the backs of her knees hidden

under the denim skirt she sewed herself. Ankles exposed as
she hovered over the electric stove. I never learned her name,
the neighbor, a twenty-year-old Mumkje so thin her wrist
bones bulged as she drew her hand

up to her mouth. Jaw sharpened to a point. She was just a
few years older than us, from Chihuahua. Never paid her
rent on time and left her youngest daughter in the same
diaper all day while her husband worked

on a well drilling crew. Not quite legal, he was always paid
in cash. One day we peeked from behind the curtains, as we
dried the supper plates, unable to avert our eyes from her
screams in Plautdietsch at her son, about

to start kindergarten, riding his bike on the dirt pile between
the two houses. *Look close, Leah said, no inner tubes, only
strips of rubber stuffed with rope. My dad says that's how the old
time Dietche still do it in Mexico. If*

we were English we would have already called CPS, but mom says we have to help our own so they don't get deported. Lips clasped, barefoot and hair tied back under her Düak with a bobble, the young Mumkje

clenched a stack of mail in her fist. Sitting straight-backed at the kitchen table across from us she stared down at the ground, cracked and floral and Leah ripped the tops off the envelopes, hieroglyphs rising from her lips.

Still in the Land: Mexico, 1970s

Dee räden nich frädlich, oba komen met faulsche Beschuldjun-
gen opp jäajen de Stelle em Launt. Psalmen 35:20

A rainbow beach ball smacked the uncovered
arms of barefoot dietsche teens from Campo 22,

Junges and Mejalles old enough to work but not
to get married, gathered every Sunday after

church in the summer, behind Pete Friesen's shed
across the path from Johnny Thiessen's rows

of apple trees on the way to Campo 10. No sand
or net, just an open pasture and Waylon Jennings

playing on a battery powered eight track. So loud
that no one heard the crack against the horse's back

or the crunching of the preacher's buggy behind them
until he grabbed Anna Fehr by the wrist as she jumped

and stretched out her palm to spike the ball. Her best
lavender dress fluttered up over her hips and before

she could reach down to cover her thighs, her face
smashed into the dirt. The eight track still screamed,

but nobody moved as the ball rolled toward the road.
the preacher sprinted. Soot colored coat flapping against

the knees of his black Bekjse as he snatched the ball out
of the ditch. Shouting, he raised the rainbow globe above

his black hat before he thrust a screwdriver into the plastic
skin. It didn't pop, just shriveled up, but they knew

he wouldn't stop until the land was quiet. He walked away
in silence: Waylon Jennings crushed beneath his tall black boots.

A Warning to Mejalles Too Young to be Waitresses

Dietsche en Mexico say that Dietsche
en Seminole are in sin, they're met Welt.

Once you cut your braids, its mat Welt
the neighbor's lips twist, met Welt.

Diewel! lines under the eyes,
death metal on the wrist, met Welt.

Inflatable beach balls and English
songs and sun bikini bliss, met Welt.

If your ears are ringing someone is
talking about what you did, met Welt.

Sin is in the heart and the mind
but especially in the hips, met Welt.

Mejalles stay at home because
the boys only want to kiss, met Welt.

Oba! Those who leave never
come back, but are missed, met Welt.

We are a people who wander but to
wander from wandering, that's met Welt.

Village Mechanics and the Mennonite Cowboy

Alfonso Herrera Sanchez Pareja, La colonización
menonita [1974]:

con pocas herramientas hacer

florecer la tierra. los menonitas no

se llegan lejos por

lo incómodo

que resulta

el constante golpeto

del hierro

sobre terreno macizo.

Mennonite Cowboy: Seminole, Texas, 2008

Cornelius Klassen parked his pop-up trailer in his son's backyard
    after he was declared dead for the second time

on an operating table in El Paso, Texas, raised, like Christ,
    ribs thrust upward as he gasped his first breath,

again. Popping open his kjnipse Hamd to reveal the incision
    to his grandchildren. Skin stretched over

the thin metal box implanted just beneath the collar
    bone. A machine, but not like the tractors he used to

haul on his semi over the mountains in Chihuahua. Air
    compressors, diesel engines, anything second hand

Mennonites bought at auction. After he got the pace-maker
    put in, he couldn't make any more bets

with his social security checks. No more scratch offs or pick six,
    beer or cigarettes, because he wasn't allowed to drive

anywhere (though his son kept tags on his '85 Cadillac,
    no air in the tires, just in case he got better). Easy chair

slumped, undershirt and boxer shorts. Not knowing his grandson
    at the Farm Supply would have snuck him Mega Millions,

tall boys and Swisher Sweets to share in the bag of Big
    Macs he brought when he dropped by to recite *The*

Education of a Wandering Man. Lined across the spine. Pulp
    westerns stacked on Cornelius' night stand.

Stories that surprise like the sharp crack of a Winchester
and move like the lonely howl of the wind across

an empty plain on the long ride home.

Village Mechanics, Revival: Manitoba Colony, Chihuahua, Mexico, Late 1940s

Freizeit, such a fun time. Summer ends with a crunch
of Rollküchen and cool Rebus on the tongue. Thick

Mumkjes swat flies, pretending not to notice the Junges
and Mejalles sneaking to the shop behind the house. He called

her schmock Me'jal and she watched him caress
the buttons of a second-hand accordion. Cowboy

hat tilted back like Antonio Tanguma. Rey
de acordeón. El mero mero de las sierras. *Tú eres*

mi media naranja. That's Spanish for my other
half. Playing "El Naranjo." Her favorite. He learned

it in the cantinas while his brother hustled eight
balls into corner pockets and his cousin, fist rattling, screamed

he would smash the skull of the next Mexa who talked
shit about Dietsche. They stuck with him the first time

he saw her. Out on the road for Sunday bunching. Pony
tail smacking against her hips while she walked arms locked

with a brood of Village girls. Mennonite cowboys, thumbs stuck
in starched belt loops. Swaggering, Kjnipse undone.

Schloabeksje slung across apple branches. Weltmenschen
on a Straum Mumkje prowl. Cherry Mooss cheeks whispered

to one another behind closed fingers. Eyes averting bodies
defined by sweat. Before snatching a second look. But Maria,

eyebrows raised, stared at Kjnals and tilted her neck
toward her parent's Somma Stoowe. He nodded, slipping

a cigarette between his lips. Smoke rising in the darkness.

***

He said the Catechism. A few drips of water
splashed on his hair, freshly cut by his mother

on the front porch. Apple faced, his sisters
whispers boom behind cupped fingers, we saw

Kjnals walking with a girl after church. Shaking
the hair from his collar he shrugged, but later

that year he knelt next to Maria
at the front of the Old Colony Church. Their backs

turned to the entire Village. Her black wedding
dress grazed his sleeve, dark, for denial

of self, as he reached for her hand, their fingers
interlocked while the Bishop rambled. He remembered

the streams that ran down her back. Spotting her
baptism dress. Bride of Christ white. He peeked

during the closing prayer and saw the empty
wall behind the pulpit. Light splashed along the edges.

Village Mechanics, Resistance: Manitoba Colony, Mexico, 1969

[George Kroeker, Unofficial Poet

    Laureate of the Mexican Old Colony

(In Exile), Circa 1969]:

[Calvin Wall Redekop, Dr., and resident Mennonite

    ethnographer, speaking

        on his behalf, will be live (from Goshen College)

in translation] *Yes, there is no sin*

        anymore a man can't

find today. [with the intention of retaining

        meaning over form] *However, if*

someone's tractor wheel has rubber around it,

        [monitored through self-surveillance] *soon*

        there is judgment.

Village Mechanics, Rebellion: Manitoba Colony, Mexico, Early 1960s

Katechismus: oder kurza und einfache Unterweisung, a brief
instruction for young people, in the form of questions

and answers. When a brother in the church has made
a misstep, how are they to be dealt with? *The evangelischen*

Bann. Church discipline. Its withdrawal and application.
If he neglects to hear or lives in gross sin,

what should be done with such a person? *The Lord Jesus*
Christ gave to his church the keys of heaven to bind

and set free and commanded that all annoying
or vexing and disobedient members of the church should be

banned from his love and the church. In order to improve those
who have become separated from the church they must be kept

apart and shunned. In this way they will be ashamed, not
for destruction of the banned, but rather, for penance and

conversion of disgraced and crushed hearts. After he has
become truly penitent it is sufficient, that he was punished

by many. Kjnals, you better make sure you don't come back unless
you've repented in front of the Jemeent and drive

out the Dieiwel. The Old Colony Bishop snipped. Preachers and
from the Village nodded, hushed and unanimous, but fingers still

outstretched in his face, because he said he'd never stop. Driving
semi-trucks to make a living. The third person this year

and it's only February. *Otherwise, you're going to hell.* At least
that's what they wrote on the paper. And spat

behind his back. Spatsearen in the feed store and the frutería.
Derjch dee Bloom fe'talen. Freizeit whispers. Silent

visiting days and Sunday lunches. No hoonsbrooden or warm
buns. Rhubarb jam, Kjnipsebrat or knocking

zoot. Sugar cubes or bitter coffee. *Kjnals was*
wiekjlerich. Too much for his own good. The Lord will hold him

accountable for what he knows. Somebody should have snapped his
will. A strong rod. A submissive child. Everyone knows

he's selling tractors with rubber tires. He spent too much time in
Mexa shops and bars. Worldly women who left

their hair uncovered. Now it's too late. Es ghet zu wheit. He has
gone too far. Dietsche speak through the flowers. He didn't

need to read it. Everyone already understood. En Kjokjebaun.
Excommunication. Thrust into his open fist.

***

When Cornelius left his truck he had a whole pack of Marlboros
stashed inside the glove compartment. That's when he saw

John and Dave, yellow nailed, coughing, Schloabeksje
dusted with smoke. They didn't run, but waited

for the snap of his belt, with the eagle buckle. Or a hand
across the seat of their pants. Could he still even spank them

if he was never home? He called them over to sit beside him
on the semi's running board, and said, Junges, be good. Go

to church and learn your catechism. *Try hard in school*
so you won't be ignorant. Listen to your mother. She is

a good woman. Ne scheina Frü. Too many tears. You don't
want to end up like me. Let's go for a ride. Climb up boys.

Village Mechanics, Rendezvous: El Paso, Texas, Late 1960s

Martha polished the bottom of the pitcher. Hips pressed
against the register. Metal hoops swinging as she whistled

at the cowboy nursing his last Tecate. At the end of the bar. A
regular. Small time pool hustler. Tapped his boot to jukebox

corridos. But didn't dance when the banda played on Saturdays.
Slammed whiskey those nights instead. His face

refracted in the mirrors as he walked towards her. *Hey Güero,
¿por qué hablas bien el español?* Balanced on the stool

across from Jesus peeking out her cleavage. He laughed. *Nací en
México. Vivía allá en el otro lado por toda mi vida.*

*Hasta ahora. No manches, Güero. ¿De dónde eres? No pareces
mexicano.* Tracing the ring around his beer, he smiled. *Sí,*

*puro mexicano. Chihuahense. ¡No chingues güey! En serio.
Soy de Cuauhtémoc. La tierra de los menonitas. ¿Menonita?*

*¿Cómo los queseros? ¿En ovrols? Sí, pero no soy quesero. Soy
troquero. Y esta ropa me pone más guapo. ¿No?* Shaking her

bouffant she laughed. *No pareces menonita tampoco. ¿Si eres
menonita porque estás aquí? ¿En un bar en El Paso?*

His hat drooped and he tipped back his Tecate. Chewing
his lips. *Es complicado.* Martha touched her chin to the counter

and fingered the brim of his knock-off Stetson. *¿Como te llamas, Güero?* Cornelio. *Dime algo en alemán, Cornelio.*

¿Algo Dietsch fe'talen? Du bas schmock Me'jal. Ne scheina Frü. ¿Qué significa eso? Solo voy a decirte si vienes conmigo.

She smiled. Red and white beams splashed against her eyelashes as he reached up and touched her cheek.

Village Mechanics, Redacted:
The Wilderness 1971

Between Sunland Park, New Mexico, and Villa Ahumada, he ran
out of gas. Again. Alone in his sleeper he pushed Honest

Abe into the Wicked Winnings
slot machine. Just one last time. Before he warmed up

the semi's diesel engine. Logged his load and headed south
toward Cuauhtémoc. Toward crisp apples and warm

bread. Ten pairs of feet. Bare for the summer but soon in
stockings and boots for the harvest and hog boiling. Except

the pig pen was empty this year. Only a few old hens.
Mare struggling to pull the cart to Saturday market. No

noise on the CB until the next morning. Palm raised
against the sun. The expanse of asphalt in either direction

while mirages reverberated beneath the Sierra Madres *¿Adónde
vas hermano? El Paso.* He waited. Thumb outstretched.

*Hungry? Elmer's Family Restaurant, serving you proudly since 1959,
still has the cheapest breakfast*

*in El Paso, $1.99. Eggs, bacon, sausage,
hotcakes and an endless cup of coffee. Bring*

*the family and come by for dinner to try
our fried chicken platter for only $4.99.*

In the mood for something Mexican instead?
Our authentic enchiladas verdes have just the right

amount of spice. Whatever you choose, top it off
with our delicious apple pie and homemade ice cream

Conveniently located next to the Econo Lodge on Montana.
Open late. Truckers always welcome.

Village Mechanics, Ruins: Early 1970s

He said he would stop driving truck. Always
after the next baby. Then he said someday

the preachers will say driving is ok. Their oldest
presses against the backyard pump. Water drips

into buckets soaking diapers. Wranglers, tighty whities,
Scholabekjse and floral dresses cranked

this morning flap in the afternoon wind. Mending
socks and missing buttons before supper. Alone,

with six mouths outside yanking weeds
from the wheat and shoveling out the chicken

coop. Two more at her ankles. Schaubelen gurgling on the
stove and a kick inside her gut.

Clots, thick, behind her that night as she stumbled, womb
open, toward Quinta Lupita. Shaking

the oldest children awake. She breathed. *Watch the
Junges. I'm going to walk to the hospital. I'm not*

sure when I'll come back. Waxing moon only conjured shad-
ows on the caliche path. She waved her arms

into the headlights of a passing truck. *Jesucristo, señora, ¿qué le
paso?* She clutched the mass

contracting under her night dress. Silent. As the man lifted
her up into the front of his pickup.

*This passport is the property of the government of
Canada. A Canadian citizen is a British subject.*

*In the name of Her Majesty the Queen
to whom it may concern, allow the bearer to pass*

*freely without any hindrance and afford
assistance and protection as may be necessary.*

Maria watched the flash pop for the second
time in her life after Cornelius decided

to hire a smuggler to sneak the kids and her
over the border. Last time she clasped a hand

over her mouth. Shocked her cousin hid
a camera in his house. Newly engaged fingers,

locked, popped open. Red faced, she raised
her ear from his shoulder. Tightening her Duäk

and swatting her dress, she shifted away from Kjnals's grasp.
Now, the passport maker in Cuauhtémoc didn't

need to tell her not to smile. She already knew what
to say when Cornelius came back. *Do you want us*

*to be stuck inside somebody's trunk? With a stranger?
Duat mindt nush, "it's expensive." He makes good papers.*

*We're not criminals. We're going to Canada. The right way. No
excuses.* She remembered when she decided

she didn't need his permission. The orchard sagged with the
first year's harvest. The boys making apple

boxes from old pallets for extra pesos. John Letkeman said
we can have them packed up in my truck by tomorrow

I'll haul them to market and bring back your share. Eight years
before she packed the last dirt around the saplings. Staked

and tied trunks against wind storms. In the spring she
snaked a drip hose row by row. Bucket feeding trees

out of reach. Snapping leaf masses every summer. But it was
only business when Cornelius came home. There were

no pigs, chickens, or apple trees as far as he was concerned.
The first years there was no fruit. The next years, they were

small and sour. But last year she squatted and pointed
upward so Dave could see. *Now, son, we have been faithful*

and the Lord has given us a harvest. But Cornelius
appeared. Raging off a South Dakota haul. *Get those apples*

*off that truck. I'm not going to pay Jake Letkeman when I can
take them into town myself.* He peeled off the yard

with a whole semi load. Orphan apples cast under the mud
flaps so he could slam the trailer shut. Three nights later his

headlights sprayed her face where she prayed in the kitchen.
The boys didn't run to meet him but kept the covers

over their heads as his boots crunched against the concrete.
Maria screamed *Where's the money Kjnals?* He answered.

Just above a whisper. *That's none of your business.* Reaching

over she smoothed her youngest's hair and looked
at the camera. *Be still, Trudy. Make a serious face. Good. A frown.*

Village Mechanics, Resignation: Ontario, 1975

After the children got finished flipping
the light switches on and off and running

water from the faucet. Smashing snow
in each other's faces. Riding bicycles

and arguing in English. Official Landed
Immigrant Status. Duäks folded

in her bottom drawers. Nude
lipstick. Home permanent and new

pairs of slacks. Maria thought
Cornelius would come back and live

in Canada. With the family. Maybe work with his brother.
Roofing. Be home for supper

or at least for Hoonsbrooden. Sunday family gatherings.
Rotary phone cord wrapped

around her knuckles, spatsearen with her sisters
in Mexico. *Tina told me Jake Loewen saw him*

at The Border Truck Stop. Hauling a John Deere
and a Mexa woman swinging from his side mirror.

Village Mechanics, Redux: El Paso, Texas, 2007

He looks up and sees the roof strained under the weight
of even just a few raindrops that he catches with five

or six metal buckets inside the house. No wonder
Martha left after his second heart attack, taking

all her Vicente Fernandez records, George Jones
eight tracks, Tigres del Norte cassettes. Intocable

CDs. Even before she moved in with her daughter, he played
solitaire down at Border Machinery. Middle-Aged Mennonite

men deal with all the heavy equipment now. Village mechanics
and business men raised up by their fathers to drive

truck. He sold them his last machines to pay off
his gambling debts. Before he lost another accordion

and ten thousand in Vegas. Cash from his brother to start
a new business. They let him hang around. Slurping

coffee and smashing cigarette butts. He fingers the machine
under his skin and presses his hearing aid against the receiver.

***

Hello, this is Honey, you have reached
Elmer's. How may I help you?

　　　　　　　Yes, I know him. Oh God,
　　　　　　　　what happened? He was just

here yesterday. Oh, thank you
　　Jesus. No, I'm ok. I'll check and see

　　　　　　　if he left his cellphone. I've served
　　　　　　　　Mr. Klassen for years. He is one

of our best customers. Black
　　coffee, two eggs, pancakes, bacon

　　　　　　　and hotcakes. I was just afraid
　　　　　　　　you were going to tell me

he died. You know, because
　　he has heart problems.

Village Mechanics, Resurrection: Manitoba Colony, Mexico, 2003

His brother, dressed in white, chips of ice packed beneath
    his body, waiting, not able to rise until that day when Jesus

comes back to the campo. Watching water drip from the end of the
coffin, Cornelius fingers his excommunication

papers in his pocket. The Darp is different now. Mumkjes gossip on
cell phones, Mejalles jump on trampolines and preachers

drive power stroke diesels. Restaurante La Sierra Thiessen se vende piz
    estilo Menonita. Talleres almost every kilometer. Tractopartes

    Dyck. Maquinarias Friesen. Refacciones Guillermo Peters.
    Centro de Servicios Fehr. Yonke de Neufeld. Ferretería Casa

Rempel. Autos Seminuevos Lowen. Industrias Reimer. Llantera
    Klassen. Now some young men have even started to work

for narco-traffickers. Cash money. American dollars. Fat pockets
    don't come from driving trucks or tractors. Two Dietsche

tried to unload a truck full of dope at Cornelius' shop. But he shouted
    If you don't get those drugs off my property. I'm going

to call the cops. It's just business Kjnals. Don't you want to make money?
    Cornelius spat. *Yes, lots of money, but a very short life. Don't*

be afraid of honest work. I already told your boss no. I don't want to see
    you here again. At Faspa after the funeral.

his sister whispers, *Kjnals you should try to get*
        your excommunication removed. That way

when you die, you'll be, in seelich soawen,
        a state of grace. Exiled. Deported.

Excommunicated. Mennonites are
        like ants. We always find the cracks and crawl back up.

Village Mechanics, Revelation:
Yale University, 1996

Dissertation: *Plautdietsch and Huuchdietsch in Chihuahua:*

> *language, literacy and identity. The threat*
> *of excommunication no longer carries physical*

banishment. Excommunicated. Old Colonists can
remain in their homes and retain contacts. No longer

> *must a disaffected Old Colonist choose*
> *an unsatisfied life in the community or life*

in the world completely
cut off from friends and family.

> *[Bourdieu]*

what speaks is not
> *the utterance, the language*
> *but the whole*
> > *social person*
[1977]

> *once ownership seemed to be*
> *allowed by leadership there*

was a rush to purchase
cars and trucks

***

In celebration of the dedication
　　of the new Old Colony

　　　　　　church in El Valle, the sixty-seven
elders, gathered from across Chihuahua

　　　　　　for this occasion, signed below

recommend to the Elesta of Colonia Manitoba (in place of the
original excommunicating Bishop,

　　now deceased)

　　　　Cornelius Klassen, be
released from membership, lifting the evangelischen Bann and
permitting contact with

　　　　church

members in good standing

　　　　and will no longer be named

　　　　　　in the congregational records.

Village Mechanics, Reckoning:
Seminole, Texas, 2010

Services will be held today for Cornelius Klassen, 78.
His sons, Pastor Dave Klassen of Seminole and Pastor John

Klassen of Canada will be officiating. A donation box
is available in the back for anyone who would like to help

with expenses. Interment will be at Gaines
County Cemetery. Please make your way to your vehicle and

switch on your headlights. You are invited to join the family

for a fellowship meal at Sommerfeld Mennonite Church
after the funeral. Carpet seams snagged the wheels

of Maria's walker as she leaned over Cornelius' metal box.
Straw hat. Dents pressed outward. Silver bolo

and striped kjnipse Hamd. Sleeves folded across his chest.
The last time she saw him sleeping. In her apartment.

Aylmer, Ontario. After Martha left. Cornelius came
to Canada. No business. Just a visit. To see some

of his kids. Grandkids. Cousins. Sisters. Brothers.
And his wife. Standing in her doorway, shifting

his boots and fingering the frame, he asked, *Has du*
mi fa'javen Maria? Yo, Ekj koa jie fa'javen. I have forgiven you,

but it's hard Kjnals, to forget what you've done. I can't change
that, but I am sorry. Nodding, arms folded across her chest.

*Ni yo, dot nu zo gout. Well, that's good enough. You can stay
with me if you want. So you don't have to get a motel.*

*Yo, I'd like that, Maria. Come in Kjnals, I've got
some coffee on.* He spent the night. Scrunched up on her sofa.

***

Cornelius dozes. Eyelids spring with a jolt
      of light against the sierras. Cold

gaps in his jacket as he blows, palms
      pressed before striking

a match against his Wranglers. Soon
      he will ride. Ojo

de la Yegua. The campo where Maria shifts,
      blouse and skirt concealed

beneath her nightdress. She will see him,
      single ember illuminated,

above a black mare bought with cash
      from stacking crates of apples

and stoking flaming barrels in the orchards
      before icicles could form

on the branches. Raising a finger
      to her lips Maria will press

mazapán into her sister's palm. Soft,
      hand on the knob so she won't

wake her parents. She will part
      the kitchen curtains and remember

her hands locked around his kjnipse,
      the hooves of the yegua pounding

tierra colorada. The fields, infinite before
      them fanning out into darkness.

II. Village Mechanics Repurposed

Invocation

For the wound that is staying, thank you.
For the wound that is leaving, thank you.

When someone says that you are acting
met Welt, just smile and say thank you.

Anywhere blows are received and brutality
is revealed, take another please, thank you.

Don't try to fix the electric fence because
prohibido el paso need not apply, thank you.

On behalf of the municipal education board's
school of hard knocks downtown, thank you.

The assassin's bullet bends toward justice but
immolation's lighter fluid says no thank you.

The effigy is ablaze and it's coming down on your head,
for the warning and illumination I thank you.

Mujeres de Juárez who carry dead jóvenes and scream
no más sangre, Santa Muerte says, fuck you.

For all those who left before me and to those who
stayed after me I will always be grateful, thank you.

Self-Portrait on Montana Street
Passing La Voz Que Calma El Desierto Iglesia Pentecostes
at seventy miles per hour

I still feel the sting of your black
blood clinging to my callouses. I tread

above you not knowing what lies
beneath the desert. While I was

wide-eyed, shaking, you revealed yourself
to me. An oilfield flare flickering,

180-West. I stood, palpitations rising
from your white and yellow lines, stretching

far beyond my red blinking light. I let
you lead me Montana,

past Little Albuquerque
past Happy's with the missing "p"

past Victory Center Homeless Shelter
past eight-dollar haircuts from Abel

past Patsy Cline and the California Raisins
past the Halfway Bar and the half-finished house

past Fiesta Adult Video Supercenter
past Lee Trevino, Joe Battle, and George Dieter

past Beer and Flats Fixed Here. Past Guadalupe
pass. Blessed be. Black tie that binds.

Mennonite Border Crossing: Bridge of the Americas, El Paso, Texas

Leife, in the passenger seat, blank, as the border guard
shuffled through my papers. Tapping his boot against
the asphalt, the officer looked up, stopped rustling
and repeated. *Sir, state your nationality and present your
papers.* Leife inhaled and pursed his lips. Our eyes met for a
moment before the guard, reclining against the side mirror,
inched down his sunglasses and seized the window molding
in his fist. *Sir, I need you to comply with my directions.* I
turned to Leife. A couple Plautdietsch syllables escaped
before the guard hissed, *I didn't ask you—you're already cleared
for transit to Canada unless you keep talking.* Hands shaking,
Leife unzipped the duffel in his lap, Ziploc stuffed with
documents crackling. *Why didn't you give me these before?* He
can't speak English, I spluttered. It's his first time crossing
the border. He needs someone who can speak Spanish. Span-
ish? He tightened his eyes at Leife. Sure as hell doesn't look
like it. ¿Hable Ud. Español? The guard snapped over my
seatbelt. Leife nodded, Sí, me llamo Levi Martens Friesen
y soy de—raising his arm the officer cut him off. ¡Abre la
cajuela! ¡Se dije, abre la cajuela! The Ziploc smashed against
the steering wheel plastic grazing my wrist as Leife begged,
Por fa', él no habla Español. You don't speak Spanish? What
are you doing in a car together if he only speaks Spanish and
you only speak English? Pull over. Get out. Both of you.

El Amor Prohibido El Paso

If you have a light, stay outside,
no smoking allowed, prohibido el paso.

Creating a nuisance on the platform
is strictly forbidden, prohibido el paso.

Alien hunting in area 51, the government
says no, conspiracy theory, prohibido el paso.

Check your local listings this show is not
available in all areas, prohibido el paso.

Alien hunting in Arizona, the government
says yes, no tres passing, prohibido el paso.

Do not pass go, do not collect 200 dollars
go directly to jail, prohibido el paso.

This is America and we speak English,
Spanish is strictly prohibited, El Paso.

Maria, an American Citizen, to Her Husband_____ Seminole, Texas, March 19th, 2011

I hereby declare, an oath,
that I absolutely and entirely renounce

and abjure all allegiance and fidelity
to any foreign prince, potentate, state

or sovereignty of whom or which I have
heretofore been a subject or citizen.

Maria spins the American flag between her fingers, New
Citizen Certificate pressed

against her knees. Her husband shifts
gears, smacking his chew. *Don't think*

I won't, wo-man. As he spits
into an empty Dr. Pepper can. She would

have bitten her lips yesterday, and maybe
will tomorrow, but today she speaks. *You*

can't talk to me that way anymore. I'm
an American citizen now and the Migra isn't

going to take my green card away. I can
vote just like you. He turns his head

and spits again, lifting an eyebrow, but
she keeps speaking. *You never let me see*

my sister and always tell me I'm too stupid
to take GED classes. But I'm not

a good-for-nothing bitch. I can
put on red lipstick and go to Wal-Mart

if I want. You aren't the boss
of my life anymore. As he begins to raise

his hand from the steering wheel,
she pauses. And remembers. The night

he smashed her face into the carpet. Broken
teeth and blood on the floor as he ripped

the tacones off her feet and set them
on fire in the front yard. She watched

the flames rise above the roof as he covered
the sparkles in lighter fluid. And came back

inside for her leather jacket and Mariah Carey
CDs. *'What else you got wo-man?'* he pounded,

'Nothin'. Because you ain't nothing
but shit.' Jaw cleched. Truck handle

pressed. She breathes. *Pos, do it if you think*
you're a man. Now I can do whatever I want.

Driving Instructions for the Tierra de las Tres Culturas

Don't go to _____.
    That place is a Narco town.

Don't take the turn-off at Villa Ahumada.
    Strange things have been happening there.

Don't go through the mountains.
    Take the 45 straight to Chihuahua, even though it's longer.

    Last time we went the other way, the militares blocked
    the road and made us pay a lot of money.

Don't go near _____.
    The fiscalía is always finding bodies there.
    It's a border between the territories and the malvados use it
    as a dumping place for their executions so their rivals can see.

A year ago, the Corredor was really dangerous. Especially
    at the intersections. That's where the balaceras happen.
    A 7-year-old in a school bus got hit with a stray bullet,
    but he lived, thank God.

    That's how the malandros fight for territory,
    but they worked it out and it's fine now.

It's ok to drive to Jagüeyes now.
    For a long time, the Narcos had it blocked.

    They'd let you through if they knew you,
    but most people didn't want to take the chance.

Stay off the Corredor.
       There was a balacera near Casa Rempel.

Stay off the Corredor.
       There was a balacera near the Telcel.

Swift is ok now. Last year they shot up the side of the Cruz
       Roja in 101. Nobody got hurt. It was fine.

Are you going north to Sabinal or Casas Grandes?
       Good. If you change your mind, don't drive between
       there and the border to get back to the States.

       Cross at Santa Teresa or Presidio instead,
       it can get really dangerous up there.

Lo que se ve no se pregunta: Campos Menonitas Chihuahua, 2018

Lo que se ve

        en el campo

Lo que se ve

        en la calle

Lo que se ve

        en la farmacia

Lo que se ve

        en el cine

Lo que se ve

        en Rubio

Lo que se ve

        en Cd. Juárez

Lo que se ve

        en Cuauhtémoc

Lo que se ve

        en Las Sierras

Lo que se ve

        en el camino

Lo que se ve

        en la rutera

Lo que se ve

        viernes por la noche

Lo que se ve

        en la carretera

Lo que se ve

        en la cervecería

Lo que se ve

        en el banco

Lo que se ve

        en el Coppel

Lo que se ve

en el OXXO

Lo que se ve

en la nevera

Lo que se ve

por la ventana

Lo que se ve

en el armario

Lo que se ve

en la cama

Lo que se ve

en los brazos

Lo que se ve

en la mirada

Los Narco-Menonitas

Border agents realized they were encountering an unlikely breed
of drug smuggler. BBC News, 2009

I.
Como hemos podido observar el problema
fundamental de los menonitas es precisamente
la falta de asimilación a nuestra comunidad
social y política.
       [La colonización menonita, 1974]

II.
Herman Sawatsky keeps no less
than $20,000 in cash stashed
under his mattress and there

is more he buried in a toolbox next
to his shed. I watched him hide
the rolls of hundreds that time

when me and my brother dug his well
a couple months ago. His wife will be
home tonight. Tuesday is not a day

for visiting. I'll knock, but wait
until I am inside. That way
she won't know what's coming.

III.

He says he heard
it on the Mennonite radio, one of those

Saturdays he was listening
to jokes that aren't funny

in English, singing along to hillbilly
gospel songs with a German

accent, that there are blonde haired, blue eyed
men in CERESO prison,

narco-menonitas from Chihuahua,
Junges with cell phones and gold

teeth. And even old Mumkjes,
hollowed out Bibles filled with
marijuana.

IV.
Meth, coke, and dope stuffed into hollow
compartments carved into queso menonita,
muebles hecho por la mano en Durango,
and oversized semi tires seized by customs
officials at the Bridge of the Americas and
Peace Arch International Park.

V.
Sus nuevas generaciones han nacido
aquí. Son mexicanos. Pero pretenden vivir intergrados
como un grupo extraño. Es necesario que cumplan
integramente con su calidad de mexicanos.

VI.
Abraham Harms went out like any good padrino
would, como el Jefe, de los jefes. Super 40Flowmaster,

treads flying off the custom chrome of his Pontiac
Firebird at 150 kilometers an hour. Smashing

his face first into the ditch as the Cuauhtémoc
police came to collect their mordida.

VII.
The fishermen saw the flowers first, satin
glints stuck in the net, as they struggled
to load it into the boat. Fabric dripped,
rotten colors through tears in the mesh

and a black shoe thrust out and slapped
at their legs. Then, a hand, bloated
and split open fell out onto the deck.

Santa Muerte Drives a White Escalade (Con El Bandido Generoso) [líbrame de males—pasados, presentes y futuros. . .]

El Vaticano no creyó
que fueron santos y no quiso

canonizar. Los santos de los que hablan
fuera de la ley. Llevanme con bien

a mi destino. Ángel de los pobres,
Señora de las sombras. Skin

stretched over hollows, mirrored
sunglasses conceal. Tinted wind

shield. Narco-corridos boom
on shattered speakers. Silent music

only she can hear. She drag
races sola through strings of red

Christmas lights, spinning tinsel
tires. Picking up hitchhikers, cholas,

soldiers, lawyers, babies, viejas,
vatos, maquileras y Jesús

Malverde at the S-Mart in Anapra
and more souls twinkling in the valley

below. Cristo Rey. *Políticos y altos*
jefes también tienen su altar. La Muerte

swerves between ruteras, past checkpoints,
federales and roadblocks. *La Patróna
está en todos lados.* Over mountains
to the minefields. What remains
of old war games. Unexploded earth. Door
handles rattle. Reaching for power
locks as she accelerates. Sonic bang
into searchlights. Beaming.

Emma Goldman Falls in Love (with Tolstoy) at the End of the World

> *If there won't be dancing at the revolution I'm not coming—E.G.*

> *Such chances arise, and they alter and direct a man's whole life—L.T. "After the Dance"*

Yes, he is a pacifist, but does he believe
      in dancing? I don't know

            if I could love a man
            opposed to both war and dancing.

Would I choose a man, like my other
      men with their hands on the trigger,

            bracing themselves for the end of the line
                  dance, over this man

with empty hands with open
      hands? Not a word

            to say about dancing, except that once
            while drunk, he watched a soldier

beat a man to death. With nothing
but his hands. And he still remembers

            how the flies circled the body. The mass
            of blood, after the dance.

Those Who Stayed

Consumed by the earth those who stayed.
Jealous of Babylon's whore those who stayed.

Not absent but never existed. Not could
have been, but never was, those who stayed.

All the ex-pats got evacuated, but the ones
who are loved are those who stayed.

Samaritan, untouchable, too poor to be
captive, exiles of exile, those who stayed.

Heretic sucked into the turbines of rapture.
to the pious contempt of those who stayed

still waiting to be
                    raised up *from glory*

to glory

            to glory

                    to glory.

Village Mechanics, Repurposed: El Paso, Texas, 2012 _____ Migrant and Refugee Center, El Paso, Texas

Saguaros loomed over a corpse. Face down in the desert. Humanitarian Aid Is Never a Crime. No More Deaths. Poster, secured to the vent with masking tape. While we waited, I winced at coloring book pages splattered across the fridge. Backwards Bs and Ds and Rs and Ss announcing their owners in crayon.

I turned to watch the braid slap against the volunteer's biker jacket as he bent to record our sack of clothes into the donation log. *Klassen?* Contorting his lips into a question mark. But then his teeth emerged from under his mustache into a belly laugh. *Imagine that!* He slapped his jeans. *Klassens here. I'm a Klassen too.* Isaac. He stood and stuck out his hand. *The Tall. Everybody calls me that. To tell me apart from all the other Isaac Klassens.*

We played The Mennonite Game to see if we were related. *I'm from Manitoba. Winnipeg area, but I was born in Mexico. Swift Current Village. Raised up in the Old Colony. Back in the old days. Horse and buggy. No electricity. It wasn't for me. Went up to Canada to work with my brother. Building houses. Got my GED and became a special education teacher. Now I'm retired.* He paused. *And divorced.*

Leaning against a scrap of paper nailed into a room divider, words from La Misa Campesina penciled on top (Yo creo en vos, cristo obrero/ Creo en vos/ arquitecto, ingeniero/ artesano, carpintero/ albañil y armador/ Porque estás vivo en el rancho/ en la fábrica en la escuela/ Creo en tu lucha sin tregua), he listened as Jon explained the Mennonite in us.

Seminole? Yeah, I've got some relatives in Seminole. My cousin works at the machine shop on Lamesa Highway. Most Mennonites there aren't pacifist anymore. Americanized. Want to drive big trucks and carry big guns. Settle down and get fat pockets. Not everyone, but it's still a shame. It's happening in Canada too. I know, it's easy to get sucked into and I made my share of mistakes.

These days I can't stay in one place too long. Thirty years in one town was long enough. I'm nomadic now. Like our ancestors. Not just Mennonites, but all the way back to the first humans. To move. To migrate. That's what it means to be alive. Even if it's just a little bit.

Oscar Romero and the murdered Maryknoll sisters peeked over his shoulders, as he asked, *You heard of Shane Claiborne and The Irresistible Revolution? Sustainability and New-Monasticism?* Jesus, indigenous. Electric blue crucifix. At the center of the campo centroamericano painted above the in-take desk. Si Me Matan Resucitaré en Mi Pueblo. Awaited our answer. Before we could part our lips, Isaac chortled. *Of course, you have, you have hair just like him! What's that called? Dreadlocks. You two look like hippies wandering around downtown El Paso.*

Nicene Question

Do I believe
in the black masked Zapatista
toting an automatic rifle Jesus?

That beret wearing Marxist
huddled in the trenches
a la izquierda con Che Guevara?

What about free love
infinitely chill acid droppin'
acoustic rockin' Jesus?

What about ninja pirate Jesus,
or Jesus in a tuxedo
t-shirt at a Def-Leopard concert?

Or pseudo-historical Jesus
who didn't really exist, except
on paper? Or pop psychology

Jesus raising my self-esteem
with that feel good religion?
G.I. Jesus giving us some

of that old-time nationalism?
Demythologized Jesus who didn't
rise from the dead, but still can be

a savior, metaphorically speaking?
freeze dried Jesus, just add water?
Do I believe in Jesus Christ

Superstar, do you think you are
who they say you are? American
Dream, cul-de-sac, stock portfolio

suv and cell phone Jesus? Do I believe
in Christ crucified? One holy Catholic
and apostolic church? Son of Man

come again to judge the living
and the dead and his kingdom
will have no end? Do I believe

in post-modern Jesus
deconstructed, in accordance with
the scriptures? Social-Darwin

Jesus who leaves the weak at
the mercy of the strong?
Apocalypse Now and napalm
J
esus, flaming tongue and
laser guided missile eyes?
My own, personal Jesus?

Certificate of Excommunication: Testing the Spirits since 1987!

Did I ever tell you about how I got kicked out of church? Not the Mennonite one—I never joined up with them. That was my mom and dad. And some of my brothers and sisters. I'm talking about the one I started going to with some Brothers and Sisters from A.A.

Well anyway, they told me to get lost. Don't come back. I didn't do nothin' but ask that preacher why he skipped a whole verse when he was reading Scripture. At Wednesday night Bible study. I didn't shout him down from the pulpit on Sunday mornin'. But he asked me if I was going to repent. Can you believe that? Said I challenged his spiritual authority in front of other believers. Grieved the Holy Spirit. But he was willing to forgive. If I asked him.

They typed up a bunch of fancy words to try to get rid of me. And sent it to our house so they didn't have to look me in the face. *Insubordinate. Sower of discord and disunity. Given over to a reprobate mind.* Whatever all that means. Look at this here. Signed by the preacher, his secretary, and all those suck ups he called elders.

Frank Dyck is hereby removed from the membership rolls of the Assemblies of God Church, Seminole, Texas, and may only return upon the review of his spiritual condition by this committee. At such time it will be determined if he demonstrates a genuine spirit of submission and repentance.

I got it framed and put that verse at the bottom so I would remember who's really the boss of me. Don't let no man act like he's God over you. *Test the spirits to see whether they are from God because many false prophets have gone out into the world!* First John 4:1. Hallelujah!

And you know what? Fifteen years later they felt bad and asked me if I wanted to come back. Guess where I told them to stick that.

La fiesta de los excéntricos: algún lugar en Los Campos Menonitas de Chihuahua (a nosotros, los queridos excéntricos en los Dietsche Darpe y el mundo entero)

Vengan las raras y los raros de Los Campos. De Chihuahua.
De La Sierra. Del mundo entero. Vengan los artistas y los

músicos. Vengan los escritores, los poetas y los fotógrafos.
Vengan los que hablan plautdietsch, inglés, y español.

Vengan los que hablan alemán, portugués, y rarámuri.
Los que hablan un poco de todos. Los que no hablan nada

de estos. Los con lenguas mezcladas. Vengan las mamás
solteras, las oole Me'jalles y las divorciadas. Vengan

los amanerados, mariposas, y mandilones. Vengan
los ateos y los católicos. Vengan los aleluyas y los ex

tradicionales y los que no sepan lo que creen. Vengan los
licenciados y los sin credencial. Los que leen y los que no

pueden. Los que viajan y los que quieran. Vengan
los malcriados, los traviesos y los mal educados. Vengan.

Vengan todas y todos. Pero solo si tengan mentes
abiertas y grandes corazones. Vengan a comer Zweiback

y Schenkenfleisch. Tacos y carne asada. Lewewarsch
y huitlacoche. Queso Menonita y tripitas. Vengan

a tomar cafecitos y fumar cigarrillos. Vengan a tomar
unas copas. Vengan para el soot

knocken y para chismear. Para contar y cantar.
Para reír y sonreír. Para soñar y soñar y soñar.

Para hacer relax. Para sentirse a gusto.
Para sentirse libres esta noche y para siempre.

We Have Gone Too Far: Self-Portrait with George Kroeker [from Calvin Wall Redekop's 1969 Ethnography The Old Colony Mennonites]

Your brother is as good as you
        For he also has his burden of sorrow
                In the same measure you do---George Kroeker

I.

We are told what to do
        Even if it is unreasonable.

II.

Schluszgedict.

Your end of day recitation.

Poetry inside the Old Colony.

Schoolhouse.

Weak was our reading and also weak was our figuring, writing

and singing. Our worthy Bible, Catechism and primer and the

Testament alone should be our books. High learning and foreign

languages have already caused much harm. Amen. But you,

George, wiekjlerich, learned enough.

Probably too much.

Now you're hoatlierich, hard of learning.

There is only one truth.

Je jeleata, je fekjata. The more you learn, the more confused you are.

In reading the Old Colonists place more importance on form than

meaning. He has written and distributed many poems in the villages.

Old Colony Poet.

An oxymoron.

Wuat est daut? What is that?

Something that shouldn't be.

But is at the same time.

III.

Soon there
        is judgment.

IV.

I don't know what you'd make of me.

From the future or maybe the Diewel.

An apparition of what happens after tractors get rubber tires.

After an Engalander marries a Dietsche.

I have rings on my fingers and in my nose and ears.

But it's alright; I'm a pacifist.

I don't like makeup and I wear a lot of flowers.

Last winter I helped slaughter a pig.

And I eat Grüewen on toast.

If you came to our house, I'd probably make you lasagna,

stir-fry, or refried beans instead of Werrennikje.

If we came to your house, your wife and I would fill your

glass, butter your bread and eat after the men.

Except, of course, *George Kroeker lived apart from his wife.*

Alone at the edge of the Village. *A bit peculiar.*

Ostracized. A result of his deviant behavior.

Maybe.

Now.

If I reached across the table, you would extend the pitcher.

V.

Obey what we have made
Or stand in shame tomorrow!

VI.

I don't know what you'd make of us, Weltmenschen, the
Jonathan Klassens of West Yandell Street in the People's
Republic of Sunset Heights.

My husband is not just any Dietsche, but an Alpha-sibling,
the oldest of ten.

A rebellious one.

His grandfather's blood—an Old Colony semi driver.

Excommunicated the same year your poems were published
in Redekopp's Appendix.

He's the son of David, a respectable preacher who teaches
the Catechism and holds marriage seminars once a year in
the Mennonite colonies in Belize.

And visits undocumented Dietsche behind glass in El Paso.

But Jon smokes Pall Malls and drinks Pabst Blue Ribbon
while listening to Howard Zinn.

Maybe someday he'll be an ethnographer like Calvin Wall
Redekopp.

But better.

Calvin translated your poems into English and didn't publish the originals.

Translation by the author, with intention of retaining meaning over form.

VII.

We are now in such a time
        That a man hears

Es Geht Zu Weit!"
        "It is going too far!"

VIII.

Jon says he's forgotten his father's mother tongue.

But he laughs in all the right places while he watches a Twilight trailer some guy in Manitoba dubbed in Plautsdietsch.

And he still asks, *wuat the shunt goen met daut?*

When his transcription software quits working.

Shouting, *wol, sheetaree* when he's pissed off.

I tell him to stop because I'm afraid of what will come out of my mouth at dietsche family gatherings.

Because Ekj woight nich Dietsch.

Well, at least not very much.

Except.

Ekj woa a Wal-Mart forn.

Schloop schein.

Zoot knocken and besupen.

Although, once I went to a Trajchmoaka and paid her five dollars.

To rub Wonder Oil on my back.

To crack my spine.

To straighten me out.

IX.

Yet where is it going?
          Forward or backward?

That which was unknown earlier
          Is forbidden out of hand.

X.

Hoy, no hay mucho Dietsch fa'talen in El Paso.

Except for two Mennonite girls who skipped past us in Family Dollar.

Pom poms for the ride back to Cuauhtémoc flapping above their matching dresses.

While we crouched between toothpaste flavors, their mother frowned at two brands of American hand soap.

Without looking up.

XI.

Must we always seek
our Salvation in the things
that will perish and will not
remain?

XII.

Once, we saw an Old Colony man at the bottom of Guadalupe Pass.

Pine Springs rest stop.

Halfway between El Paso and Seminole.

He hitched up his overalls and straightened his John Deere

cap as he walked back toward his semi. An end loader

strapped to the back. Placas de Chihuahua.

Raising a work glove, he greeted us in the only language

he thought we'd recognize.

Buenos días.

Smiling, he chuckled.

Silver tooth beaming in the sun.

Plautdietsch (Low-German) Glossary in Order of Appearance

Grösspapa- grandfather

Dietsche- literally "German," used as a Mennonite identifier

Kjnpse Hamd- western-style shirt with snaps

Bekjse- pants

Die Biebel- the Bible

Engalander- English (non-Mennonite)

Mumkje- literally "Mother,"used as a title for a married woman

Mejjal/le- girl/s

Jung/e- boy/s

Schekbenjel- literally "errand boy," used to identify a young man low in the working hierarchy

Darp/e- village/s

Smokje/Schmauk- pretty/beautiful

Sommabarsch- summer borscht

Gröpe- a large pot

Grüewen- pork cracklings

Trajchmoaka- literally "bonesetter," used to identify a traditional healer

Duäk- traditional head covering worn by married women

Taunte- aunt

Faspa- a meal that is traditionally eaten after church or holidays that typically consists of cheese, pickles, bread, sausage and baked goods

Kringel- a twisted breadstick often served on special occasions

Kjielkje- noodles

Plautdietsch- Low German

Met Welt- worldly

Diewel- devil

Oba!- Oh dear!

Freizeit- literally "free time," often to signify fun events for young people that coincide with church activities

Rollküchen- a desert made with fried dough, typically served with watermelon

Rebus- watermelon

Mexa- used to refer to Mexican people, derogatory in tone

Schloabeksje- overalls, identifies men from the most traditional communities

Weltmenschen- worldy people

Cherry Mooss- a whipped dessert made with cherries

Somma Stoowe- literally "summer room," often used for receiving guests

Katechismus- Catechism

Oder kurza und einfache Unterweisung- a brief instruction for young people, in the form of questions

Je'meent- community

Spatsearen- to talk

Derjch dee Bloom fe'talen- literally "to speak through the flowers," used to make allusions to topics not discussed and to speak in a way where someone knows to read between the lines

Hoonsbrooden- a traditional dish made with chicken

Wiekjlerich- literally "easy of learning," used to identify someone who picks up on information easily

Es ghet zu wheit- it has gone too far

En Kjokjebaun- excommunicated

Ne scheina Frü- a good woman

Schaubelen- beans

Duat mindt nush- that doesn't matter

Seelich soawen- state of grace

Huuchdietsch- literally "High German," differentiates the
German spoken in Germany from Mennonite Low-German
(Plautdiestch)

Elesta- bishop

Evangelischen Bann- church discipline

Has du mi fa'javen?- Have you forgiven me?

Yo, Ekj koa jie fa'javen-Yes, I have forgiven you

Schluszgedict- daily recitation in school

Hoatlierich- literally "hard of learning"

Je jeleata, je fekjata- the more you learn, the more confused
you are

Wuat est daut?- what is that?

Werrennikje- traditional cottage cheese perogies covered in
cream or strawberry sauce

Wuat the shunt goen met daut?- what the hell is going on?

Wol, sheetaree- well, shit

Ekj woight nich Dietsch- I don't speak (Low) German

Ekj woa a Wal-Mart forn- I'm going to drive to Walmart

Schloop Schein- sleep well

Zoot knocken- cracking sunflower seeds

Besupen- drunk

Acknowledgements

I want to express my deepest gratitude to the village across three countries who made this collection possible. Thank you to Sasha Pimentel and the UTEP Bilingual Creative Writing MFA class of 2013 for guiding this manuscript in its infancy stages. Thank you so much to early readers including Susan Lampley, Leah Shelton, Veronica and Marcela Enns, Anna Wall, and Kerry Fast and a special shoutout to everyone who gave feedback the manuscript's use of Low German. Thank you to everyone who participated in the 2018 Rebels, Exiles, and Bridge Builders oral history project in the Tres Culturas Region of Chihuahua, which further helped contextualize the events that frame this book. Last but not least, I want extend an enormous thank you to everyone who shared their memories and family stories, especially the Klassen family who has offered intimate perspectives of a family and community in transition. Thank you to my husband Jonathan without whose love, support, and encouragement this book would not be possible. Thank you to my children Luna and Sage who give me hope for a better world.

This book is dedicated to those who endured pain and hardship in familiar and unfamiliar lands and to those who continue to navigate a flood of convergences in guise of commonplace.

Publication Credits

"Walking in Colonia Rubio," "Self-Portraits with the Flower Women," "Neighbor," "Still in the Land," "Divine Healing," "A Warning to Every Mennonite Waitress in Mexico," "Thoughts while Driving West out of Seminole, Texas," "The Schekbenjel Goes for a Ride," and "Watching Las Reinas," were originally published in *The Center for Mennonite Writing Journal.* "Lilies of the Field" and "Rite of Passage" originally appeared in *Rhubarb.* "Sonnet for Tobacco Pickers" was originally published in *ZYZZYVA.* "Mennonite Border Crossing" originally appeared in *Anthropology and Humanism.* "Temporary People" was originally published in *Guernica.* "Thriftway Run" originally appeared in *Cimarron Review.* "Self-Portrait on Montana Street" was originally published in the *Rio Grande Review.* "Los Narco-Menonitas" originally appeared in *Huizache.* "Chupacabra Summer" originally appeared in *Hobart.* "Nicene Question" originally was published in *Geez.* "Maria an American Citizen to her Husband _____" originally appeared in *Barrio Panther.* "Emma Goldman Falls in Love (with Tolstoy) at the End of the World" was originally published in *Matter.* "Santa Muerte Drives a White Escalade" originally appeared in the *Goodbye Mexico: Poems of Remembrance anthology.* "El Amor Prohibido El Paso" originally appeared in the *New Border Voices anthology.* "Village Mechanics and the Mennonite Cowboy" was originally published as "The Wandering Heart of Cornelius Klassen" in the *29 Mennonite Poets anthology.*

Abigail Carl-Klassen is a poet, writer, researcher, educator, translator, and activist living in El Paso, Texas, with her husband and two children. She grew up in the oil fields of the Permian Basin alongside Old Colony Mennonite immigrants from Mexico and has worked in education, language services, community development, social science research, and agriculture in a variety of contexts across the U.S. and Latin America. She earned an MFA in Bilingual Creative Writing from the University of Texas at El Paso and her work has been published widely in English and Spanish, appearing in *ZYZZYVA, Catapult, Cimarron Review, Guernica, Aster(ix) Huizache,* and others. She has published two poetry chapbooks, *A'int Country Like You* (Digging Press) and *Shelter Management* (dancing girl press) and is the winner of the Boungavillea Prize. Recordings of her oral history project, "Rebels, Exiles, and Bridge Builders: Cross-Cultural Encounters in the Campos Menonitas of Chihuahua" can be found on the Darp Stories YouTube channel.

www.ingramcontent.com/pod-product-compliance
Lightning Source LLC
Chambersburg PA
CBHW020422130626
46549CB00006B/2688